MUMFORD & SONS

SIGH NO MORE

WISE PUBLICATIONS
part of The Music Sales Group

London/New York/Paris/Sydney/Copenhagen/Berlin/Madrid/Hong Kong/Tokyo

Published by
Wise Publications
14/15 Berners Street, London W1T 3LJ, UK.

Exclusive distributors:
Music Sales Limited
Distribution Centre, Newmarket Road,
Bury St Edmunds, Suffolk IP33 3YB, UK.

Music Sales Pty Limited
20 Resolution Drive, Caringbah, NSW 2229, Australia.

Order No. AM1000714
ISBN 978-1-84938-570-1

Original CD designed by Studio Juice.
Photography by Max Knight at Pimpernel & Partners.

Edited by Jenni Wheeler.

Printed in the EU.

www.musicsales.com

SIGH NO MORE

Words & Music by Marcus Mumford.

Love, it will not be-tray you, dis-may or en-slave you, it will set you
There is a de-sign, an a-lign-ment, a cry, of my heart to

free. Be more like the man you were made to be.
see the beau-ty of love as it was made

to be.

to be.

to be.

THE CAVE

Words & Music by Marcus Mumford.

13

Verse 2

The harvest left no food for you to eat,
You cannibal, you meat-eater, you see.
But I have seen the same,
I know the shame in your defeat.

Verse 3

'Cause I have other things to fill my time,
You take what is yours and I'll take mine.
Now let me at the truth,
Which will refresh my broken mind.

Verse 4

So tie me to a post and block my ears,
I can see widows and orphans through my tears.
And know my call despite my faults
And despite my growing fears.

WINTER WINDS

Words & Music by Marcus Mumford.

18

But my____ heart told my head:__ "This time

no,__ this__ time____ no."____ We'll be

washed and____ bu - ried____ one__ day____ my____ girl. And the time we were

giv-en will be left for__ the world.__ The flesh that lived and loved will be

But my___ heart told my head:_ "This time no."_____

And my___ head told my heart:_ "Let love grow"_____

But my___ heart told my head:_ "This time no, this___ time___

___ no."_____ Oh._____

ROLL AWAY YOUR STONE

Words & Music by Marcus Mumford.

yet it dom - i - nates the things I see.

But you, you've gone too far this time, You have neith-er rea-son nor rhyme with which to take this home— that is so right-ful-ly—— mine.

WHITE BLANK PAGE

Words & Music by Marcus Mumford.

1. Can you lie next to her and give her your
2. A white blank page and a swell-ing

lov - ing_____ you with my whole_____ heart?
fol - low_____ you with my whole_____ life.

I GAVE YOU ALL

Words & Music by Marcus Mumford.

D.S. al Coda

But close my eyes for a while.

And force from the world a pa-tient smile.

But I gave you all._____ I gave you all.____

_____ I gave you all.____

LITTLE LION MAN

Words & Music by Marcus Mumford.

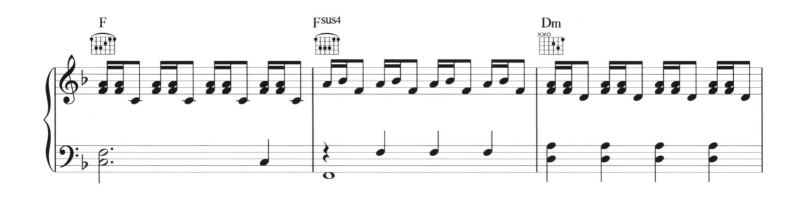

2. Trem-ble for your-self, my man, you know that you have seen this all be - fore._____

did-n't I   my___ dear?___   Did-n't I   my___

___ dear.

Ah_____

Ah_____

But it was

not your fault, but mine.___ And it was your heart on the line.___ I real-ly

TIMSHEL

Words & Music by Marcus Mumford.

1. Cold is the wat - er,_____ it free-zes your al - read-y cold
(2.) you are the moth - er,_____ the moth-er of your ba - by

THISTLE & WEEDS

Words & Music by Marcus Mumford.

62

I will hold on. I will hold on.

AWAKE MY SOUL

Words & Music by Marcus Mumford.

weak-ness I feel I must fi-nal-ly show.

D   A^sus4   D

2. Lend me your hand and we'll con-quer them all.   But
𝄋 fick - le my heart and how woo - zy my eyes.   I

A^sus4   D

lend me your heart and I'll just let you fall.   But your
strug - gle to find an - y truth in your lies.   And

A^sus4   D

Lend me your eyes, I can change what you see.   But your
now my heart stum-bles on things I don't know.   My

bod - ies____ we will live. In these bod - ies____ we will die. And where you in - vest____ your____

love, you in - vest____ your____ life.

♩ = 120

73

DUST BOWL DANCE

Words & Music by Marcus Mumford.

dust - y bar-ren land__ had giv-en all it could yield.__
now I am sure my heart can

2. I've been

nev - er be still.__ So col - lect your cou - rage and col - lect__ your horse and

pray you nev - er feel this same kind of re - morse.__

Seal my heart and break_ my pride. I've no-where to stand_ and now no-where to hide._ A-

2° instrumental

-lign my heart, my bod-y, my mind to face what I've done_ and do my time._

Play 4 times ad lib.

-lign my heart, my bod-y, my mind to face what I've done__ and do my time.__

Drums cont. sim.

Instr. ad lib.

Oh, yes sir, yes sir, yes it was me. I know what I've done_'cause I know what I've seen.__

I went out back and I got__ my gun. I said "You have-n't met__ me, I am the on-ly son."

AFTER THE STORM

Words & Music by Marcus Mumford.

mind and not this heart, I won't rot.
hold with all I have, that's why I hold.
And I took you by the
And I will die a-

hand___ and we stood tall.
-lone___ and be left there.
And re-
Well, I

-mem - bered our own land,___
guess I'll just go home,___
To Coda
what we live
or God knows

for.
But

there will come a time, you'll see, with no more tears. And love will not break your

heart but dis-miss your fears. Get o - ver your hill and see what you find there. With

grace in your heart and flow - ers in your hair.

D.S. al Coda

85

C Em G C Em
love will not break your heart but dis-miss your fears. Get o - ver your hill and
G C Em G
1.
see what you find there. With grace in your heart and flow - ers in your hair.
2.
G
flow - ers in your hair.
rit.
D/F♯ G

2 3 4 5 6 7 8 9